ARCTIC ANIMALS

Bobbie Kalman

The Arctic World Series

Toronto
New York
Crabtree Publishing Company

The Arctic World Series
Created by Bobbie Kalman

Editor-in-Chief:
Bobbie Kalman

Writing team:
Bobbie Kalman
Janine Schaub
Liz Hart
Christine Arthurs
Ken Faris

Managing Editor:
Janine Schaub

Editors:
Liz Hart
Christine Arthurs
Susan Hughes

Design:
Heather Delfino
Maureen Shaughnessy
Stephen Latimer

Computer layout:
Christine Arthurs

Printer:
Bryant Press

For Josephine and Philip

Special thanks to: Ken Faris for his groundwork in the series; John Livingston for his expert advice; Berit Qundos for tracking down Lapp reindeer photos in Stockholm; Robin Brass for his desktop publishing advice and linotronic output; Arnie Krause for his continuing patience and support.

Cataloguing in Publication Data

Kalman, Bobbie, 1947-
    Arctic animals

(The Arctic world series)
Includes index.
ISBN 0-86505-145-3 (bound) ISBN 0-86505-155-0 (pbk.)

1. Animal ecology - Arctic regions - Juvenile literature.
2. Zoology - Arctic regions - Juvenile literature. I. Title.
II. Series: Kalman, Bobbie, 1947- . The Arctic world series.

QL105.K34 1988   j591.52'621

350 Fifth Avenue
Suite 3308
New York
N.Y. 10118

120 Carlton Street
Suite 309
Toronto, Ontario
Canada M5A 4K2

Contents

A jaeger takes flight into the crisp arctic sky.

A cold, cold world

The biting winds blow their chilly message across the land. Snow and ice cover the ground in an endless white sheet stretching as far as the eye can see. There are only a few hours of daylight now, and soon it will be dark again. Winter has returned to the Arctic!

Most of the creatures that have spent the summer here are now gone. Only a few permanent residents remain. The animals that make the Arctic their year-round home are a rugged bunch, but even though they are strong, small changes in the environment can mean starvation or death for them. What is it like to live in the Arctic year after year? How do birds, fish, and mammals manage to survive?

Darkness and ice

In the winter, not only is the arctic land dark, the Arctic Ocean is pitch black, too. Ice covers the surface of the water, and not many of the sun's rays are able to penetrate the ice. With the lack of sunlight, only a few plants are able to grow in the dim underwater world.

The Arctic comes back to life

When spring arrives, large areas of ice melt, and the sun's rays are able to shine into the water. Simple plants called phytoplankton begin to grow, using the sun's energy and important nutrients that have been collecting in the water all winter. Soon the open water is full of phytoplankton. Tiny water animals called zooplankton graze on the phytoplankton. Zooplankton are then eaten by other sea creatures such as fish, shrimp, and whales.

Plentiful waters

Millions of birds fly to the Arctic during the summer to feed on the rich supplies of sea creatures that teem in the ice-free waters. Different kinds of whales also migrate to the Arctic's food-rich waters for the same reason. Many land animals that normally live farther south, such as some species of caribou, travel great distances to find food on the tundra. They graze on the shrubs, flowers, and grasses that are plentiful in the summer months. The Arctic becomes a large summer resort for hundreds of species of birds, mammals, and fish.

Constant daylight

Just as there are endless hours of darkness during the winter, the opposite is true in the summer months. In some areas of the high Arctic the sun never sets. Even in the more southern regions there are as many as twenty hours of daylight. Having so many hours of daylight gives animals more time to breed, find food, and build up their strength. At the end of the short summer the waters freeze once again. The visiting animals leave the Arctic in great numbers; only the arctic residents remain to face the challenges of winter.

Keeping warm

How do animals that live in the Arctic manage to keep out the chilling cold? There are several ways in which these animals have adapted to the severe environment. Animals with cold blood, such as frogs and snakes, would freeze to death because their body temperatures depend on the surroundings in which they live—so, one of the features of all year-round arctic land residents is warm blood. Having warm blood assures birds and mammals of a constant body temperature. Other features such as thick hair, a layer of fat, and feathers help keep the body heat of certain arctic animals from escaping.

How does hair help animals stay warm?

Many of the fur-covered animals that live in the Arctic have two layers of hair. The layer of hair next to the skin is short, densely packed, and soft. This layer is known as ground hair, underhair, or underfur. The outer layer of hair, called guard hair, is long and bristly.

Both layers of hair are coated with an oil produced by a gland located at the base of each hair. The oil from these glands helps waterproof the animals by repelling any water on their fur. It also helps keep animals warm by trapping a layer of air next to their skins. In the same way storm windows insulate our homes, this air cushion helps keep the cold air from reaching the skins of arctic animals.

Hollow hairs

Some arctic animals have hollow hairs mixed in with their other fur. These hollow hairs also keep body heat in, and they help animals stay afloat in the water. Polar bears and caribou both have hollow hairs. Polar bears spend much of their time in the water hunting seals, and caribou must often swim across wide rivers during their migrations.

Changing coats

When summer comes, the fur-bearing animals shed their winter coats for lighter summer fur. The colors of the summer coats often change as well. These coats are darker to match the gray-brown shades of the tundra.

This boy's husky has two layers of hair to keep it warm.

How does fat protect mammals from the cold?

A person can easily die after spending only a few short minutes in icy water because human beings are not adapted to such freezing conditions. Arctic animals, though, are protected from the cold by large stores of fat found just beneath their skins. In marine mammals this fat is called blubber. Blubber does not allow an animal's body heat to escape during cold temperatures. Many arctic land animals have layers of fat as well as thick fur coats to keep them warm.

How do feathers keep birds warm and dry?

Most of the birds that live in the Arctic year round have two sets of feathers. The ptarmigan and snowy owl are covered in feathers from the tops of their heads to the tips of their toes! How do their feathery snowsuits keep these birds warm? A soft layer of down found next to their skins keeps the birds cozy, and their oily outer feathers keep them dry.

A bird spends hours each day caring for, or preening, its feathers. It uses its beak to pick up oil from a gland that is located above its tail. It carefully spreads this oil over each feather from base to tip. When birds preen, they also take great care to arrange their feathers in such a way that the hooks, or barbs, of each feather overlap. Water runs off these overlapping feathers in much the same way overlapping roof tiles keep the rain and snow out of a house.

A hunter is pulling the skin off the seal that he has caught. The mass of white tissue under its skin is a thick layer of insulating blubber.

The ptarmigan is so well suited to arctic life that even its feet are covered in feathers.

The polar bear

Splash! With one powerful leap the polar bear dives into the chilly Arctic Ocean. Swimming from one ice floe to another, he soon drags his heavy bottom out of the water once again, shakes the water off his thick, white coat, and rolls in the snow to dry himself off. With a sniff he might check the frigid air for the aroma of a seal. The polar bear is the largest arctic land-living carnivore.

Designed for traveling

The polar bear can travel hundreds of kilometers with a steady, bandy-legged gait. Wide paws help this bear walk on snow and swim in water. Furry soles keep it from slipping on the ice, and partially webbed feet make this animal a strong swimmer. Polar bears have been known to swim out as far as one hundred kilometers from shore!

A mighty hunter

The Inuit have always respected the polar bear for its expert hunting abilities. A strong and patient bear can stalk and kill a seal with one mighty swat of its paw. Polar bears hunt year round, but most females stay in a den with their cubs for several months in the winter. Although seals are definitely a polar bear's favorite meal, these bears also eat a great variety of other foods such as berries, seaweed, grass, eggs, garbage, and even the occasional beluga whale.

Thick layers of fat and fur make the relatively cool arctic summers seem hot to polar bears. As a result, polar bears are less active in warmer weather. They are most active during the spring hunting season.

A polar bear's paw is so powerful it can kill a seal with one blow. Notice how wide the paw is. This helps the bear walk on snow and swim more quickly.

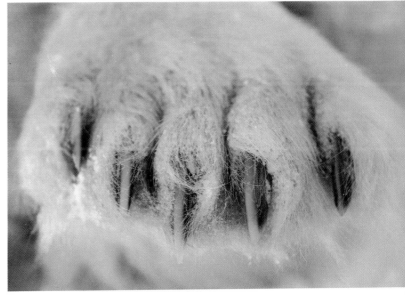

Too warm in summer

A thick layer of fat, a dense coat of underfur, and coarse, hollow guard hairs help keep the bear toasty warm. This mighty mammal is so well adapted to the cold that it feels uncomfortable in warm weather. With built-up stores of fat from spring seal hunting, this huge bear lies around for most of the summer.

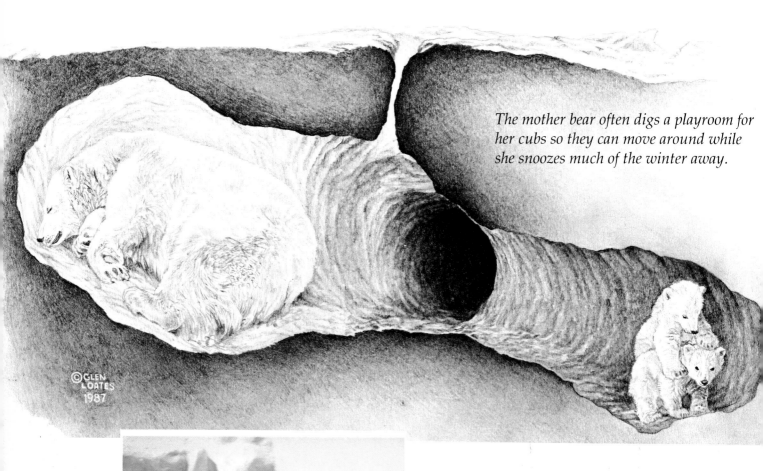

The mother bear often digs a playroom for her cubs so they can move around while she snoozes much of the winter away.

Helpless cubs

An adult polar bear is a powerful animal, but a newborn cub is completely helpless. It is so tiny, it can fit into your hand!

In October the mother bear digs herself a den in a snowdrift. Gusty winds and snowy blizzards soon cover over the entrance. She makes a breathing hole in the roof. By late November or early December she gives birth to one or two cubs. They keep warm by lying on their mother's belly or in the cradle of her forelegs. She feeds them her rich, fat milk.

Tiny polar bears nurse even after they have left the den. They stay with their mother for up to two years.

Breaking out

By the end of March the cubs are ready to say hello to their big, white world. It is time for their mother to break open the sealed den with her powerful paw, revealing a shockingly bright landscape. The cubs scamper up and down small hills of snow and test the strength of their legs. They are playful little creatures, slipping across the ice and sliding down snowbanks.

Gaining independence

The cubs are totally dependent on their mother for the first year. She nurses them and patiently teaches them valuable hunting skills. It takes them a long time to learn how to trap and kill a seal so, for up to two years, they rely on their mother for food and guidance. When the twins leave her, they usually stay together for a while. Soon they, too, go their separate ways.

Whales are mammals

It is believed by many experts that whales lived on land long ago. They were much smaller than they are today and their bodies resembled those of land mammals. Their flippers looked a lot like hands! Over millions of years their bodies changed to suit ocean life. Today whales are much larger because they live in water. Water supports the great weight of their bodies and helps keep these huge mammals cool.

Nothing fishy

Even though whales live in water, they are not fish; they are mammals. They have some hair on their bodies, and they are warm blooded. This means that their body temperatures do not change to adapt to the cold ocean waters. Unlike fish, whales have lungs, not gills, so they cannot breathe underwater. In order to breathe, they swim to the surface to take in air through blowholes that are located on the top of their heads.

Whale calves

Whereas fish lay eggs that later hatch into baby fish, whales give birth to babies called calves. Before giving birth, some whales spend the summer in the arctic waters where there is plenty of food. They move south to warmer waters, however, when it is time to have their offspring. Other whales never leave arctic waters. When they are ready to calve, they move closer to the coastline where the water is shallower and warmer.

As soon as the calves are born, the mothers push them to the surface for their first breath of air. Then it is time to eat. One feature unique to mammals is that mothers are able to nurse their babies. Their mammary glands produce milk. Whales' milk is almost ten times as rich in fat as cows' milk. This creamy liquid helps young whales grow quickly and put on a thick layer of blubber.

The beluga

Many kinds of whales visit the Arctic, but only three species live year round in the ice-filled Arctic Ocean: the beluga, narwhal, and bowhead.

The beluga, or white whale as it is sometimes called, resides along the coastline of the Arctic Ocean. It is an expert swimmer in the shallow waters of bays and rivers. Sometimes in spring belugas swim into waters that are so shallow that most of their bodies are out of the water. They do this so that they can scratch themselves on the ocean floor. The whales are itchy because they are molting!

Social singers

Belugas are unusual in many ways. They are very social and like to stay in pods. They also love to sing. Whalers used to call them "sea canaries" because they often heard the trills, moos, and screams of beluga melodies.

The beluga's white color and preference for shallow waters make this smaller whale easy to spot and hunt. Killer whales, polar bears, and people have killed many of these gentle animals. As a result, these whales are protected, and only native hunters are allowed to capture a certain number of them.

The narwhal

The narwhal is one of the most unusual whales in the ocean. The male narwhal has a long, spiral tusk, which is actually a front tooth. As this unusual tooth grows beyond normal size, it pierces the maturing whale's upper lip. The gums and lip heal around the tusk as it grows in.

Long ago, before southerners knew much about narwhals, their tusks were thought to have magical powers. Many believed that these tusks belonged to magical unicorns. When someone found such a tusk washed up on a beach, there was great excitement!

Mystery tusk

What is the purpose of the narwhal's tusk? Some people believe the tusk is used to spear fish or stir up edible plants from the floor of the sea. This theory is unlikely because female narwhals, which must also eat, very rarely have tusks. There are others who believe that the narwhal uses its tusk to battle other males for a mate or to become the leader of the pod. This, too, seems unlikely because a tusk is quite brittle and would easily break in a duel.

A healthy sign

It is generally believed that the males with the largest tusks are the dominant animals in the pod. A big tusk is a sign

At one time the washed-up tusks of narwhals were believed to be those of unicorns!

that a narwhal is healthy because a large amount of food energy is required for a tusk to grow. Perhaps the herd knows by instinct that the strongest males are the ones with the largest tusks.

Precious horns

Because the narwhal's long, spiral tusk is so unusual, many people are willing to pay a lot of of money to own one. As a result, the narwhal has been overhunted by people for many years. Now the narwhal population is partially protected by law. In order to prevent overhunting, there are strict limits on the number of narwhals people can kill in a season of hunting.

Using their heads

As a mammal, the narwhal needs air to survive. When the water becomes completely frozen over in winter, narwhals make breathing holes by butting at the ice with their foreheads. Similarly, if they become trapped when ice forms quickly on the freezing water, they use their strong foreheads to break through it. Narwhals are able to push and bang their foreheads through extremely thick layers of ice!

No dorsal fins

As other arctic whales, narwhals lack a dorsal fin. Can you guess why? How might dorsal fins interfere while the whale is swimming underneath ice?

The bowhead

The bowhead, once known as the Greenland right whale, got its name from the arctic whalers of long ago who noticed that this whale's lower jaw was curved like a bow and that its head made up more than a third of its whole body size.

Eating on the move

In summer herds of bowheads migrate north to feed in the high Arctic. In winter they travel to the southern Arctic where the water is open and slightly warmer. As they swim, they keep their mouths open and catch the sea's rich supply of food. Since they are such huge animals, it is rather amazing that these mammals should depend on tiny sea creatures for their diet. They eat tiny shrimp-like crustaceans called krill and small fish such as herrings and sardines.

A toothless giant

Some species of whales have teeth, but the bowhead does not. Instead, this whale has plates of baleen that hang from the roof of its mouth like a thick, fringed curtain. These triangular plates collect the sea's tiny creatures as the water is sifted out of the whale's mouth. Although whalebone is another name for baleen, baleen is not made from bone. It is actually made from a substance similar to that found in fingernails and horns.

An endangered species

In the old days there were no materials such as plastic or steel. Baleen, being both strong and flexible, was the only material available for making a number of useful products. This springy substance was used for fishing poles, umbrella rods, and ribs that stiffened women's dresses. The bowhead was also valued because its blubber could be melted down into oil. In those days whale oil was the best oil for lighting lamps. The flame from whale oil is clean burning and odorless.

Bowhead whales were hunted so heavily for their baleen and blubber that there are only around three thousand of them left in the Arctic. Today only native peoples are allowed to hunt bowheads, and strict quotas are being set to make sure that only a few are killed each year. No one wants to see these gentle giants disappear from the earth forever!

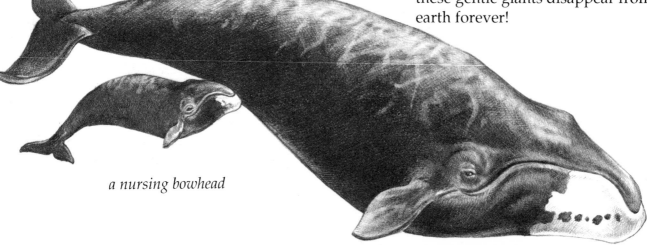

a nursing bowhead

Pinnipeds

Walruses and seals are flippered mammals that belong to the same family. The scientific name for a seal or a walrus is a pinniped. All pinnipeds are equally at home on ice, land, and in the water. Even though they spend a lot of time underwater, they breathe air just as all mammals do.

The seal family

There are two main groups of seals: seals with ears and seals with flat openings at the sides of their heads. Both types can survive in cold water, but earless seals are better suited to life in an icy environment. They have a thick layer of blubber under their smooth skins. Eared seals have a thinner layer of blubber, so they have to rely on their thick fur to keep them warm. They must keep moving in the water, whereas earless seals can float motionless without becoming chilled.

There are thirty-two species of seals in all, several of which live in the Arctic. Earless seals, such as the ringed and harp seals, spend a good deal of time there. Each species differs from the others in some ways, but they also share many common features.

Special eyes

Seals have large, brown eyes that are equipped with a mirror-like membrane at the back. This membrane helps them see in the dark ocean waters. When they are out of the water, their pupils shrink to protect their eyes from the glare of the snow. Their eyesight, however, is not very good while they are on land, making these animals easy prey for polar bears and human hunters.

Are all seals crybabies?

Tears are constantly streaming out of a seal's eyes, but this is not because the animal is unhappy. Seals cannot control their flow of tears. They spend a lot of time going into and coming out of the water, and tearing helps wash away salt water and specks of dirt from their eyes.

Yearly cycles

In the spring great numbers of seals gather in the abundant arctic waters. Females give birth to seal pups around this time. They haul themselves out onto pack ice or rocky shores when it is time to whelp, or give birth. Sometimes many females of one species whelp in the same area. This birthing place is called a rookery. A group of females, called a harem, is often guarded by a male seal.

Nursing pups

Baby seals that are born on sheets of ice are usually pure snowy white, while those that spend their early lives on rocky shores have coats of spotted gray or sandy brown. The pups stay close to their mothers, constantly feeding on her rich milk. Young seals are encouraged to become independent as early as possible because nursing weakens the mother by using up her much-needed stores of fat.

Going with the floes

While they are molting, many species of seals spend their summer months out of water. As the weather begins to turn colder, the arctic waters start freezing up. Some seals, especially those that live together in large groups, migrate long distances at this time in order to find enough food. The hardier or more solitary ones merely travel from the high Arctic to the lower ranges of the Arctic until the spring thaw once again replenishes the sea's rich food supply.

Expert divers

Compared to that of a human being, a seal's breathing system is much better adapted to long, deep, underwater dives. Some seals can dive to depths of 600 meters and remain underwater for nearly an hour! Before diving, a person takes a deep breath. When a seal dives, it expels all the air from its lungs. Empty lungs enable a seal to make deeper dives without getting a serious condition known as "the bends."

Painful gas bubbles

If a mammal dives too deeply with full lungs, a gas called nitrogen contained in the air it has breathed is absorbed by its body tissues. When the mammal surfaces, many tiny bubbles of nitrogen are forced into its bloodstream. These bubbles are always painful and often cause death. Human deep-sea divers must take precautions against the bends because they are not naturally equipped for diving as seals are.

Seals, such as this ringed seal, cut many breathing holes through the ice with their claws and teeth.

Where's the oxygen?

While it is underwater, a seal gets the oxygen it needs from the rich supply in its bloodstream. A seal can carry more oxygen in its bloodstream than many other mammals can. A large number of red blood cells carry the dissolved oxygen to the seal's heart and brain. Once the oxygen in the seal's bloodstream is used up, the animal comes to the surface for fresh air.

Under and over the ice

A seal spends a great deal of time under the ice diving for arctic cod, crab, and various other types of shellfish. Yet, the surface of the sea is often covered in ice, and the seal must always have access to a supply of air. To solve this problem, a seal makes its own breathing holes. It uses the spiked claws on its flippers and its ultra-sharp teeth to cut these holes in the thick ice. Each seal has several such holes and visits them regularly to make sure they are ice free.

In water and on land seals investigate noises and interesting objects. They are naturally curious animals and do not always flee when they see something approaching—even if it is one of their many dangerous predators. Their curiosity and poor eyesight sometimes cost them their lives.

Ringed seals

Ringed seals are the most common kind of earless seals in the Arctic, as well as the smallest. They stay all year round, swimming in the chilly waters and lying around on the ice floes. A ringed seal is well insulated from its cold world because close to half its weight is made up of blubber!

Like other seals, the ringed seal enjoys taking short naps and warming itself in the sun.

Air-conditioning flippers

The flippers of ringed seals, and all earless seals, are not insulated with blubber. To make up for this, when the water is icy cold, very little blood travels to the flippers and only a small amount of blood is cooled. Valuable body heat is not wasted trying to keep the flippers warm. In warm weather blood flows freely to the flippers. The blood is cooled in the vessels that are close to the surface of the skin. Temperature-regulated flippers enable seals to warm up or cool down their bodies!

A unique hiding place

Unlike any other kind of seal, mother ringed seals protect their pups by hiding them in dens burrowed deep in the snow. Even though the entrance to these dens is underwater, the arctic fox and polar bear can still sniff out the pups. People and animals stay far away from the dens of the male ringed seals for a good reason. Male ringed seals give off a strong, musky smell. It is so foul that the Inuit call these seals "tiggaks," or stinkers!

Harp seals are so cute that many people feel they should not be hunted at all.

Saving the cute

Seals face many dangers because they are hunted by both people and animals. People kill them for their meat, blubber, and skin. Harp seals, which live from the high Arctic near Greenland to the coast of Nova Scotia, have long been targets of commercial hunters because of their beautiful fur—especially the snow-white fur of the baby harp seals. Seal hunting disturbs many people who feel sorry for the cute and helpless baby seals, especially the adorable harp seal. As a result, strict limits have been placed on harp seal hunting, even though this animal is not endangered. Unfortunately, there are many other animals that are overhunted and endangered, yet their plight does not receive as much attention as the cause of this seal does. The amount of public sympathy felt for seals is greater than that for other animals because people find seals irresistable.

The walrus

Imagine having a tooth as long as your arm! The walrus does. Both the male and female have two long canine teeth called tusks. Tusks are not used for chewing because they are too far in front of the walrus's other teeth to be of any use. Walruses use their tusks to crack breathing holes in the ice. Hooking their tusks into ice floes helps these enormous animals haul their huge bodies out of the water. These tusks may also be a sign of social rank. The larger the tusks, the more important the animal is in the herd.

Seafood diet

Walruses are equipped with whiskers with which they feel around for food as they move slowly along the seabed. When they discover a small sea creature buried in the mud, they squirt a strong jet of water, uncovering the buried sea worms, snails, or crabs.

Thick-skinned animals

Walruses are protected from the chilly arctic waters in two ways: they have blubber under their skins, and their blood circulation automatically adjusts itself to the outside temperature. When a walrus feels hot, its blood is pumped to its blubber and skin where it can be cooled by the air or water. The cooled blood then travels through the system, cooling the rest of the animal. When a walrus is exposed to cold conditions, it is able to limit the supply of blood to its blubber and skin, thereby keeping its body heat inside.

Few enemies

Polar bears and killer whales are the only natural enemies of the walrus. They are the only animals that can chew through its extremely tough hide. Polar bears must work hard to gnaw a hole in the hide of a dead walrus. They then scoop out the insides through the hole.

Bringing up baby

A female walrus gives birth to a single calf every two years. The mother supplies milk high in fat content to her calf for the first year of its life. This enables the young calf to grow quickly. Calves leave the protective care of their mothers when they are three years old.

Walruses live in herds all around the Arctic Ocean. They lie on the ice floes sleeping and digesting their big meals.

Baby snow geese keep warm under their mother's wings.

Loons are found on land when nesting.

Arctic birds

It is June, and the air is filled with flapping wings. Millions of birds are returning to the Arctic. Many of them have traveled as far as five thousand kilometers. It seems like a lot of trouble to go such a distance when these visitors have only eight to ten weeks to mate, build nests, have chicks and train them, molt and grow a new set of feathers, and then prepare to return south again. However, with all the extra hours of daylight and abundance of food both on the tundra and in the ocean, the birds keep coming back year after year to enjoy this plentiful bounty.

Summer visitors

Summer visitors include the snow bunting, the arctic tern, and the murre, to name just a few. Only a few birds are hardy enough to remain in the Arctic all year. Some of the winter residents include the snowy owl, the raven, the gyrfalcon, and the ptarmigan.

The arctic tern

The arctic tern must love the sun because it makes an incredibly long journey each year to be assured of continual daylight! This graceful bird is the world's greatest traveler. It makes a yearly migration of over 35 000 kilometers from the Antarctic to the Arctic and back. Flocks of terns visit the Arctic each summer to breed near the coast. Sometimes they settle so far north that they make their cuplike nests right in the snow.

Major migration

After the breeding season is over, the terns begin a two-month journey to the Antarctic—the other pole of the earth. Since the Antarctic is in the southern hemisphere, this means that the terns arrive there just as the hours of sunlight are increasing. When the hours of sunlight diminish again, the terns head back to the Arctic. In just one year they have flown around the world!

The puffin is so brightly marked, you almost expect it to live in the tropics.

When the snow bunting arrives in the north, it means that spring has returned.

There are several types of gulls in the Arctic. Ross's gull is one of the most beautiful and rarely seen northern species.

An arctic tern is snatching dinner.

The murre

The murre is one of the twenty-two species of seabirds in the auk family. Sometimes people get it confused with the penguin. Although both birds are stocky and have white-and-black bodies, there are two ways to tell them apart. Murres live in the Arctic, while penguins live in the Antarctic; murres can fly, while penguins cannot. Even though murres can fly, they are not very good at it. They must move their short, narrow wings very rapidly in order to take off. They are more graceful swimmers than fliers. When they dive,

When it is time to breed, murres gather on seaside cliffs in groups called bazaars.

they move their wings as if they are flying underwater. Their powerful leg muscles and webbed feet help them swim even more quickly.

Arctic murres spend most of their lives at sea, using their expert diving and swimming skills to catch small fish, crustaceans, and mollusks. Each spring, however, hundreds of thousands of murres arrive at the land's edge. They come to breed on the seaside cliffs of the arctic coastline.

A bizarre bird bazaar

Large groups of breeding murres are called colonies, or bazaars. You may have heard the word bazaar used to describe a marketplace. A bazaar of murres certainly sounds like a crowded marketplace! With thousands of birds nesting together, there is constant activity and a deafening noise.

Pear-shaped eggs

Murres do not build nests. Instead, the female bird lays a single, pear-shaped egg directly onto a bare, narrow rock ledge. Naturally, the large number of birds on the nesting ledges results in many murre eggs being knocked off the edge. In fact, it is surprising that any eggs survive to the hatching stage. The reason that so many do is simple but ingenious: murre eggs are pear shaped. When they roll, instead of moving in a straight line towards and over the cliff edge as a round egg would, they roll in a small arc, never really moving from their original spot.

The black guillemot is another member of the auk family commonly seen in the eastern Arctic. It resembles a duck. Its feet are bright red, its bill is pointed, and it has patches of white on its black wings.

The common murre has a thin bill and white eye ring, while the thick-billed murre has a thick bill and no eye ring.

One, two, three—jump!

When young murres hatch, they are cared for by their parents for two or three weeks. Then it is time for them to go to sea. In some colonies the adult murres fly down to the foot of the cliffs and call to their young to join them. The chicks cannot yet fly, so they must pluck up enough courage to leap off the rocky cliffs into the water below. Sometimes the cliffs are as tall as city skyscrapers! The chicks jump down and swim out to sea with the adult murres. Two years later they will return to the coast, ready to urge their own chicks to take that giant leap into the sea.

The snowy owl

The snowy owl lives in the Arctic all year long. It is one of the few birds that has feathers on its legs and feet. Its head-to-toe feathery snowsuit helps insulate it from the winter cold. During blizzards the snowy owl faces directly into the storm so that the wind will press its feathers against its body. This helps the owl lock in its body warmth.

Remarkable vision

The snowy owl has excellent eyesight. Even though it often flies as high as an airplane, it can see a suitable place to land. The snowy can also easily spot its prey from above. It swoops down,

grasps its dinner, and returns to the nest. Then it rips its food into large pieces or swallows it whole. The owl's strong stomach juices dissolve the edible parts. The bones, teeth, and fur of the prey are formed into a pellet, which is later regurgitated by the owl.

Taking care of the owlets

When food is plentiful in the Arctic, the female snowy lays about ten eggs. While she sits on her eggs to keep them from freezing, her mate brings her food. The eggs hatch one by one over a period of a month. The owlets are fed and raised by both their parents. They stay in a small, shallow hole in the ground while their flight feathers are growing in. During this time, if an owlet leaves the nest, its father follows it around faithfully to protect and feed it. In eight weeks the owlets are ready to fly off in search of their own food.

Southern visits

The lemming is the snowy owl's main source of food. About once every three or four years the lemming population in the Arctic decreases. During these times snowy owls fly to southern Canada and the northern United States in search of other animal food. Birdwatchers often go to nearby airports to spot these magnificent birds. They know that snowy owls like to land in places that are as open as their natural habitat, the tundra.

The female snowy owl is not as pure white as the male. It has gray bars along its wing feathers. The female is also a bit larger than the male.

The raven

The Inuit have many legends about the raven. In fact, it seems that wherever ravens are found, folk tales have been written about them. The raven is a bird with a bad reputation! In many fables, songs, and stories this big, black bird is shown as a thief. One Inuit legend tells that the raven used to talk but, because he betrayed the trust of a snowy owl and ate the bird's eggs, he lost his power of speech and can only now make a loud "caw, caw" sound.

Cold feet

The raven does not look like a bird that could survive arctic winters. Unlike the snowy owl and the ptarmigan, it does not have extra protective feathers on its body or feet. The raven's looks are deceiving, however, because its body plumage does keep it warm in the severe arctic cold. The raven also has a natural way of avoiding heat loss through its feet. Just enough blood reaches them to maintain a temperature slightly above freezing level, thereby preventing the raven's feet from freezing.

Strong survival instincts

The raven is able to survive in the Arctic because it is an intelligent and resourceful bird. It is not a fussy eater and is extremely skillful at getting its food. After this black bird has found or stolen its dinner, it carries away the extra food in its crop—the pouch in its throat. The crafty raven takes the food to a hiding place where it is stored for future use.

The raven is sometimes called a robber because it often steals food. This adaptable bird eats almost everything, including small mammals, birds, eggs, insects, and carrion, the meat of dead animals. It eats carcasses abandoned on the tundra and leftover food from garbage dumps.

The gyrfalcon

Small animals and birds quiver when they see the gyrfalcon's shadow. This mighty bird's swift flight, sharp eyesight, and strong talons help make it an effective hunter. By flying close to the ground, this bird of prey can swiftly lock onto an unsuspecting lemming or ptarmigan with its powerful talons. The falcon can also fly quickly enough to seize a bird in mid-flight and kill it with a blow from its beak.

Depending on lemmings

In the Arctic, animal populations change from year to year. In years when there is a large supply of ptarmigans and lemmings, the gyrfalcon has no trouble finding food. If food is scarce, the gyrfalcon lays fewer eggs.

Nesting habits

Instead of building its own nest, the gyrfalcon takes over the abandoned nests of peregrine falcons, hawks, or ravens. These nests, called eyries, are usually built high up on cliff edges beneath rocky overhangs. This safe, sheltered spot protects the young birds from snow and rain.

The female lays from two to seven eggs, but the average is four. When the chicks hatch, their eyes are open, and the tiny birds are covered in down. It is a full-time job for a mother falcon to feed them. Once she arrives with a freshly killed animal, she tears the prey into pieces with her sharp beak. The chicks

This baby gyrfalcon waits patiently for its mother to return with a tasty tidbit of ptarmigan for dinner.

stay in the nest for 45 to 47 days until their flight feathers grow in. After the chicks learn to fly, their parents teach them the finer points of hunting. Then the baby falcons are ready to live on their own.

A pair of gyrfalcons often returns to the same nesting spot year after year until the nest becomes cluttered with the remains of prey. The couple then moves to a clean, new home somewhere else!

31

The ptarmigan

Changing colors

The ptarmigan is a popular prey for many arctic animals. It does not have powerful defense features such as a sharp beak or claws. Instead, it relies on camouflage to hide it from its enemies.

The ptarmigan molts several times each year. When the new set of feathers has grown in, it matches the colors of the tundra. In spring the ptarmigan's feathers are brown and yellow, resembling the spring grasses. Its wing feathers are white to mirror the few snowy patches that have not yet melted. In winter the ptarmigan molts again and, this time, its new feathers are almost entirely white. The ptarmigan's winter coloring makes this bird very difficult to spot against the snow and ice!

When the female ptarmigan sits on its nest, its summer coloring blends in with its nesting place.

The hardy ptarmigan stays in the Arctic all year, but when the long, cold winter arrives, it prefers the southern regions of the Arctic where the snow is not as deep nor as tightly packed. It seeks areas where food can be found above the snow and where it can burrow into loosely packed snow for a sleep. The snow helps insulate the ptarmigan against the cold.

Arctic adaptations

In order to survive, the ptarmigan has adapted in other ways. Its eyes allow it to see just as well in the many hours of winter darkness as in the almost constant daylight of the summer.

The ptarmigan is completely covered by warm feathers. Even its nostrils and feet are feathered to provide protection from the cold. The plumage on its feet also makes the ptarmigan's feet wider. Wide feet spread its weight more evenly so it can walk on soft snow without sinking. These feet feathers are, not surprisingly, called snowshoe feathers!

Two species of ptarmigans live in the Arctic. The rock ptarmigan inhabits the high, rocky hills and is at home on the arctic islands. The willow ptarmigan looks for more sheltered areas in the southern arctic regions. Though the two birds look similar, the willow ptarmigan is larger and has a heavier bill. The willow ptarmigans above have not yet lost their snowy white plumage. Ptarmigans are loud birds. Their noises resemble the sounds bullfrogs make.

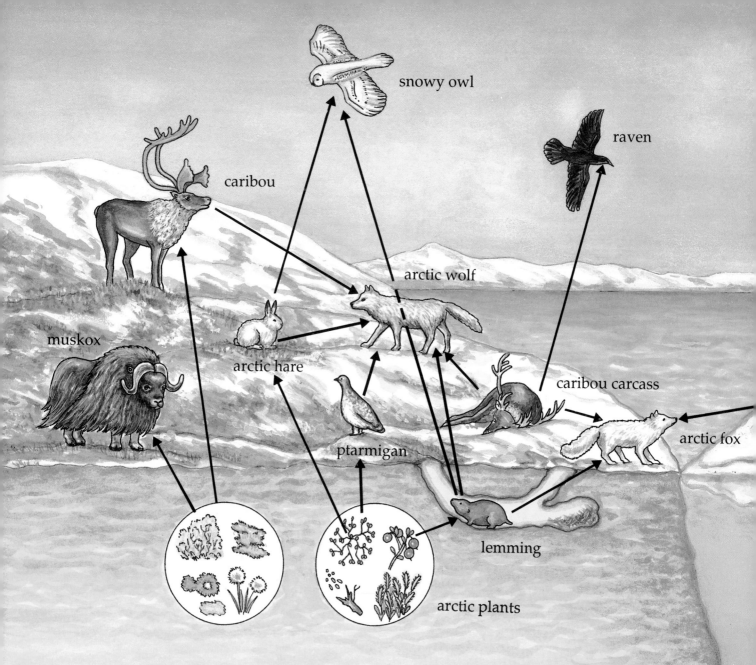

snowy owl

raven

caribou

arctic wolf

muskox

arctic hare

caribou carcass

ptarmigan

arctic fox

lemming

arctic plants

Arctic food chain

Every time an animal eats, it takes in food energy. When an arctic willow shoot is eaten by a lemming, and the lemming is eaten by an arctic fox, energy is passed along the food chain. The arctic willow, the lemming, and the arctic fox are each links in one food chain. The animals that are part of the arctic food chain do not have as many food choices as the animals living in other habitats. When food becomes scarce, arctic animals must sometimes move south to find food or in many cases they have fewer babies until their food supply is back to normal. Drastic changes in the environment, such as those caused by environmental disasters, cause certain animals to die.

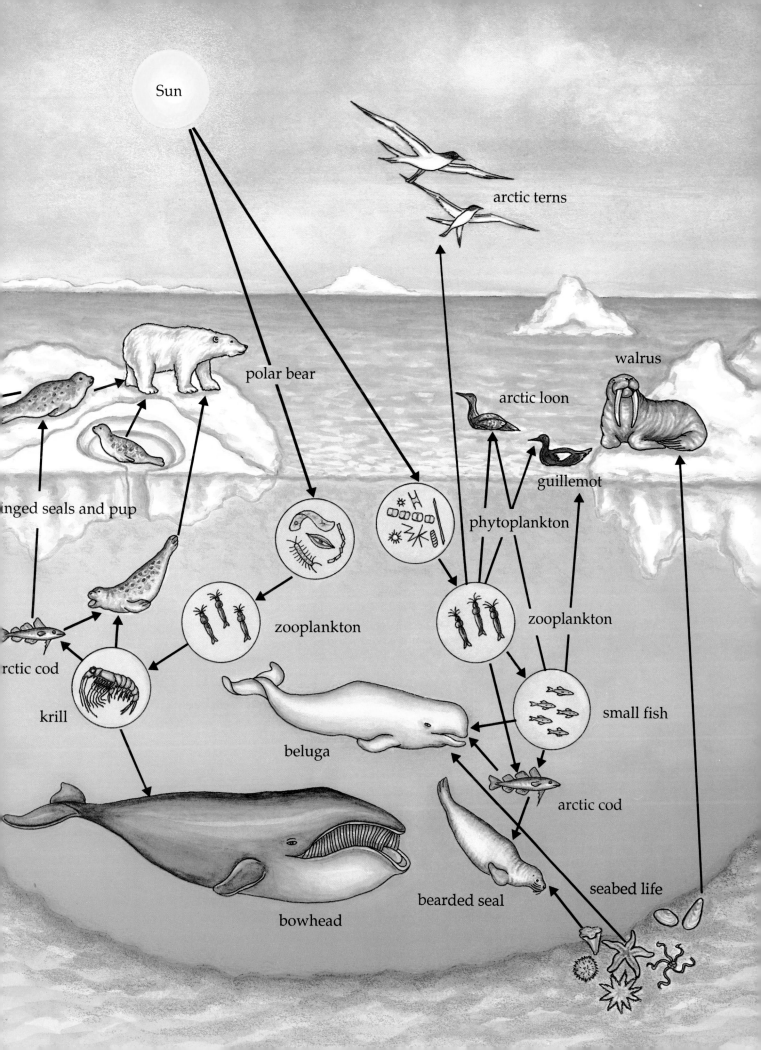

Sun

arctic terns

polar bear

walrus

arctic loon

ringed seals and pup

guillemot

phytoplankton

zooplankton

zooplankton

arctic cod

small fish

krill

beluga

arctic cod

bearded seal

seabed life

bowhead

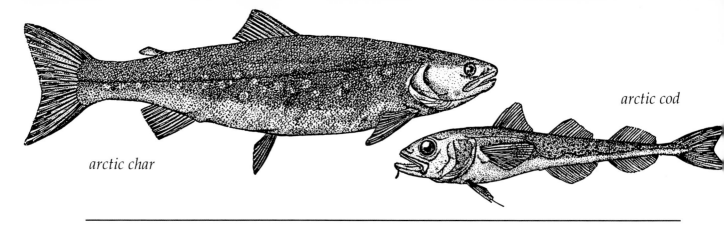

arctic char

arctic cod

Polar fish and insects

In the cold arctic waters there are fewer than fifty species of fish. The arctic flounder, the arctic lamprey, and the arctic char are examples of fish that live in the waters close to shore, while several species of fish, such as the sculpin, live near the bottoms of arctic seas, rivers, and lakes.

In the far north the arctic cod is the most common fish. It is a popular food source for people and many marine animals. The cod lives among the cracks and hills on the underside of sea ice. Its mouth opens forwards and upwards so that it can feed on the creatures that live on the bottoms of ice floes!

One might say that polar fish are quite ordinary. They do not have many specialized features because they have no need to compete with other fish for food. Most species of arctic fish are dull gray in color and have large eyes because they have adapted to the low levels of light in the ice-covered Arctic Ocean.

Arctic fish are slow to grow and mature. Their body processes are less active in the chilly waters and, as a bonus, they live longer than fish in warmer waters!

Bugs, bugs, bugs

During the short arctic summer the tundra buzzes with the sounds of insects. Moths, beetles, spiders, flies, and hundreds of other kinds of bugs make the Arctic their home. These insects have adapted well to their polar lives. Many insects are small, dark colored, and hairy. These features help keep them warm and reduce the amount of water that they lose in the polar climate. One kind of mosquito lays eggs that hatch only when there is enough water for the larvae to survive. Sometimes the eggs laid on very dry land wait up to three years until there is enough moisture for them to hatch!

Troublesome parasites

All animals that live in the wild suffer with parasites. Despite the bitter arctic cold, mites, lice, and fleas live in the fur of all arctic animals. Whales, walruses, and seals also have lice and worms. If you were able to look closely at a whale's skin, you could see the tiny tracks that the lice have left behind. Whale lice have sharp, hooked legs that make small gouges in skin! When an animal is healthy, parasites cause only minor problems. However, parasites can weaken unhealthy animals, and in the Arctic, sick animals do not live long!

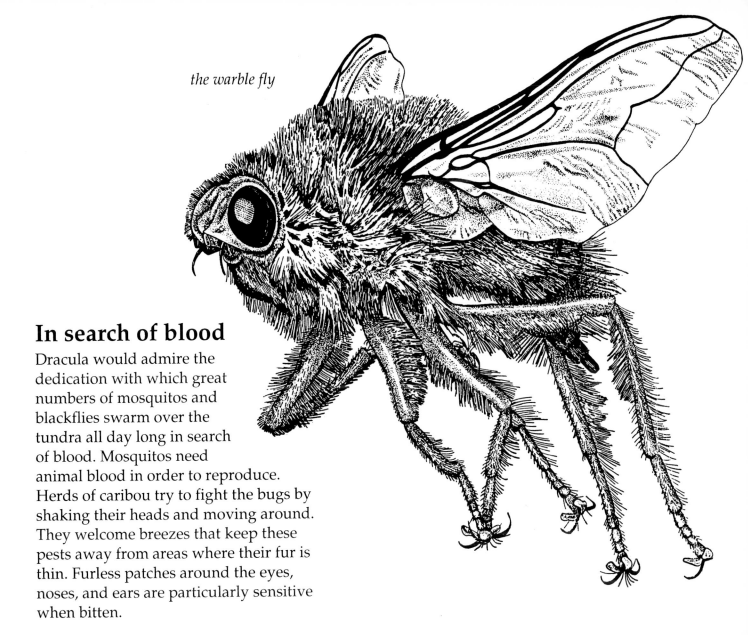

the warble fly

In search of blood

Dracula would admire the dedication with which great numbers of mosquitos and blackflies swarm over the tundra all day long in search of blood. Mosquitos need animal blood in order to reproduce. Herds of caribou try to fight the bugs by shaking their heads and moving around. They welcome breezes that keep these pests away from areas where their fur is thin. Furless patches around the eyes, noses, and ears are particularly sensitive when bitten.

Bugs using anti-freeze?

Cars that have to run in the winter must use anti-freeze in their radiators. Water in a radiator helps cool the engine, and anti-freeze prevents the water from freezing in cold weather. Some beetles have a substance similar to anti-freeze in their bodies. This anti-freeze agent is made up of sugar and protein which helps bugs stay active in cold weather.

The warble fly

Not only is the warble fly hairy and ugly, it is obnoxious. A whole herd of caribou may stampede as the animals try to escape its stinging bite!

Mosquitos cover this man's jacket as they search for a blood donor on the summer tundra.

Reindeer and caribou

For thousands of years reindeer have been important domestic animals to many arctic peoples. In Lapland, an area north of the Arctic Circle in Scandinavia, some Lapps still depend on these small, donkey-sized animals for food, hides, and transportation. When the reindeer migrate, the Lapp reindeer farmers follow their herds.

Reindeer are also important to the Chukchi, the native people of eastern Siberia. Unlike the Lapps, the Chukchi herd wild reindeer. Although the Chukchi can now buy some of their food, many still rely on the reindeer for meat, milk, and clothing.

A young Lapp herder with one of his reindeer.

40

The caribou

The reindeer found in the North American Arctic are called caribou. Caribou are generally larger than the reindeer of Europe and Asia. There are several different types. Those that live in the northern forests and migrate to the arctic tundra are the barren-ground or northern caribou. Peary's caribou live on the high arctic islands.

On the move

Each February when spring is on its way, huge herds of up to 10 000 caribou begin their long northern journeys across snow and frozen lakes onto the open, treeless tundra. Here the female caribou bear their calves. Calves are born with their eyes wide open and their bodies covered in cozy fur. They learn to walk soon after they are born because they must be ready to travel with the herd.

In the summer caribou herds wander across the tundra, feeding on grasses, sedges, mosses, and lichens. They eat as much as possible so they can live off the fat stored in their bodies when food becomes scarce during the winter months.

Antlers

Caribou are unusual members of the deer family because both the male and female have antlers. A female's antlers are smaller than a male's and are not shed until after the mothers have calved in the spring. Perhaps females keep their antlers during the winter so they can fight off males that try to steal their food.

The male caribou's shovel-shaped brow tine is used to dig through snow for hidden vegetation.

Hunted by wolves

The main predator of the caribou is the wolf. To guard against wolves, caribou travel in herds. If a wolf enters the herd, the caribou alert one another. A healthy caribou can easily outrun a wolf, so the wolves usually kill the sick, weak, and old members of the herd.

While the caribou are giving birth, wolves are also busy having babies. Caribou fawns are therefore quite safe during their first few weeks because wolves must stay close to home to tend their own young.

Peary's caribou

The Peary's caribou is a small, white, reindeer-like caribou that lives on the high arctic islands. Although these endangered caribou are protected from hunting, their numbers have been vastly reduced by a series of severe winters and ice storms. They have not yet recovered. These animals remain on the arctic islands year round, searching for food in areas of sparse vegetation.

The muskox

The shaggy muskox looks like a huge beast, but much of its size comes from its extraordinary fur coat. If you shaved off its hair, the muskox, which is a relative of the antelope, would be about the size of a small cow! Its coat traps body heat so the animal can stay warm. Under the long, outer guard hairs, there is a heavy layer of wool close to the skin. This soft woolly blanket covers every part of the muskox except its lips and nostrils.

During the winter months muskoxen conserve their body heat by crowding together in large, slow-moving herds. In blizzards the herds stop and huddle together in warm groups. Sometimes the animals lie down beside one another in the snow to keep warm and cozy.

Best feet forward

Muskoxen have hoofs that spread out when weight is placed on them. This allows the animals to walk on soft snow without sinking too deeply under their own weight. They use their sharp-edged hoofs to dig craters in the snow so they can feed on buried willows, grasses, and sedges. If the snow is hard, muskoxen break the crust by banging their chins against it.

A muskox's skirt-length hair keeps it extremely warm during the winter months.

Bull-fighting

In the late summer and autumn male oxen begin fighting. First they bellow at one another, rub their faces against their forelegs, then back up and charge. When they butt their massive heads together, their thick skulls and huge horns absorb the shock of these cracking blows. Once these displays are over, the females choose their mates.

Although bulls fight during mating season, at other times they work together to protect one another against enemies. When a herd of muskoxen is threatened by wolves, the oxen form a tight line to protect the calves. If the wolves surround the herd, the muskoxen form a circle around their calves, with their horns facing outwards. Sometimes an angry muskox charges its enemy from this position. Although muskoxen often stand still when threatened, they are able to run very quickly if they must!

Losing their underwear

In the warm summer the muskox no longer needs its heavy winter coat. It sheds its underlayer of fine fur, causing strands of hair to litter the land. Did you know that muskox hair is called *qiviut*?

Muskoxen use this effective defence formation in summer and winter.

The arctic ground squirrel

Northern peoples frequently see *sik-siks*, or arctic ground squirrels, but ground squirrels usually see them first! This curious little animal is quick to pop its head out of a hole on the tundra. It twitches its nose, stands up on its back feet, and chirps at the world.

Ground squirrels live underground in groups called colonies. They dig shallow burrows in areas where water drains away easily and build a labyrinth of connecting tunnels with several entrances so they can easily find one in case of danger. Squirrels are very sociable and enjoy sharing their huge networks of tunnels.

Fattening up for winter

During spring and summer ground squirrels put on a layer of fat in order to be ready for their long winter sleep. They eat a wide variety of food, such as tundra plants, seeds, and fruits, and begin storing this food inside their burrows in late summer. When these hungry animals emerge from their burrows in the spring, they eat their stored food until new plants begin growing on the tundra.

Hibernation dens

Ground squirrels are the only arctic animals that hibernate during the winter. They cannot find enough food to remain strong and warm, and hibernation allows them to conserve these essential body resources. To prepare for their seven-month sleep, ground squirrels build hibernation dens. These small burrows are lined with lichens, leaves, and one of the warmest wools in the world—muskox hair.

When the autumn air becomes cold, and the decreasing daylight warns of the coming of winter, the squirrels nestle in their dens. They roll themselves into balls, wind their tails over their heads and shoulders, and go to sleep. While hibernating, their body temperatures drop to just above freezing, and their heartbeat slows down. In this deep winter sleep ground squirrels will not awaken even if they are picked up. They do, however, wake naturally every few weeks to clean themselves and their dens.

The collared lemming

Lemmings are small creatures about the size of guinea pigs. They have short legs, ears, and tails to help them conserve heat. Their thick fur also keeps them warm. Their brown coats begin turning white when the first autumn blizzards strike. Collared lemmings are the only members of the rodent family that have white fur during the winter months. White fur helps camouflage them while they are foraging for food on the surface of the snow.

Seasonal homes

In summer lemmings live in shallow burrows under the ground. The burrows have resting spots, toilet areas, and nesting chambers that are lined with grasses, feathers, or muskox wool. The rooms of the burrows are connected by narrow tunnels. During the winter lemmings grow special claws on their feet to help them dig tunnels in the hard snow. They eat frozen shrubs and grasses.

In their search for new homes and food lemmings swim across ponds and rivers. Many never make it to the other side. Disease, not enough food, and attacks by predators may also be reasons for the fewer number of lemmings. The lemming is one of the most valuable links in the arctic food chain. When there are fewer lemmings, there are also fewer predators. Likewise, when the number of lemmings increases, the animals that prey on them have more babies too.

Lemming years

Every three or four years lemmings go through a cycle of overpopulation. This is followed by a sharp decrease in their numbers. No one is certain why the lemming population rises and falls in this pattern, but scientists have come up with several theories. High levels of lemming populations cause over-crowding and, as a result, these rodents stop breeding and begin looking for food elsewhere.

Lemmings must mature and reproduce quickly on the arctic tundra. Many other animals prey on these small polar rodents.

Large groups of hares live together on the tundra.

The arctic hare

Imagine a gathering of a hundred white hares on the tundra. You might feel as if you've slipped down a magic rabbit hole into a strange wonderland! Such is the high Arctic where clusters of white hares come together for warmth and protection. Sometimes up to 120 hares form a huddle on the tundra. If a wolf or a fox approaches, the hares hop away in different directions to find shelter behind rocks or in cracks. This sudden frenzy of hopping might be frightening or, at the very least, confusing to the predators of the hares.

To survive the cold, the arctic hare must adapt in ways that southern hares do not. In winter it grows a pure white coat of thick, long hair, which camouflages the animal in the snow. Its small ears help it conserve heat. The jackrabbit of Arizona has huge ears. When the blood flows through them, it helps cool down the rabbit's whole body. The arctic hare has small ears for the opposite reason. Very little blood travels to its ears, so its body does not get cooled off. Instead, short ears help the animal conserve its body heat in the cold polar climate.

Feeding habits

In summer the arctic hare eats a wide variety of plants. In winter it feeds on bare twigs and digs for vegetation just below the surface of the snow. The arctic hare will even eat meat if there is no other food to be found.

A litter of leverets

In the spring between five and seven baby hares, called leverets, are born to a mother hare. Her nest is usually a natural depression in the tundra. The leverets are born furry and with their eyes wide open. They can run within a few minutes of birth but, for the first several weeks, they cannot bound quickly enough to outrun their enemies. When there is danger, they flatten their ears against their bodies and lie as still as they can to escape being seen. Young arctic hares grow quickly during the short arctic summer. They grow twice as fast as any other type of hare!

Snowshoe feet

If you have ever tried to walk through deep, soft snow, you know how difficult it can be because all the force of your weight is concentrated onto the small area where your feet touch the snow. Wearing a pair of cross-country skis or snowshoes makes it much easier to travel across snow. Snowshoes and skis help spread a person's weight over a larger area, thereby preventing him or her from sinking down into the snow.

In the same way, the bodies of some arctic animals and birds have adapted to walking on snow. The arctic hare's large hind feet enable it to run on top of the snow. In soft snow the arctic hare spreads its toes out and makes its snowshoes even wider. The feathers on the snowy owl's legs and toes help the owl support itself on snow in the same way. The wide and furry feet of the arctic fox also allow it to run easily across unpacked snow, just as the wide hoofs of the muskox and the caribou keep these bigger animals from sinking.

The snowshoe feet of the arctic hare keep it from sinking down into the snow.

Hide and seek

Many animals rely heavily on their sense of sight to help them locate and kill their prey. The prey, however, have also developed a natural means of protection against the sharp eyes of their predators. Their coats are camouflaged to match their surroundings. Fur or feathers often change with each season as the animals or birds molt or shed their coats. In the winter some birds and animals turn white so they blend in with their snow-covered environment. Unfortunately, this natural camouflage not only helps hide the prey from the predators, it also helps disguise predators as they seek their prey!

These golden plover chicks set against the arctic tundra show nature's fascinating camouflage techniques.

No nose?

Some observers claim that the polar bear goes to great lengths to hide itself when it seeks its favorite prey—the ringed seal. Although its white fur is good camouflage, sometimes the polar bear's black nose gives the animal away. People have reported seeing this crafty predator cover its nose with its paw while sneaking up on an unsuspecting seal!

When snowy owlets hatch, their soft downy feathers are gray to match the color of their nesting area.

The arctic fox

The arctic fox is about the size of a large cat. It is well adapted to cold weather and rarely needs to take shelter, even during blizzards. Its stubby, heavily furred ears, snout, and legs help prevent the loss of its important body heat. Its extremely thick, oily fur sheds water and keeps the animal dry. Like many other arctic animals and birds, this fox changes color with the seasons. In winter it has a heavy white coat; in summer its fur is reddish brown.

The arctic fox builds a den in the light, sandy soil near stream beds or on hillsides where it is easy to dig. Foxes use some dens over and over again. A good den may be used for hundreds of years by generations of foxes.

Caring parents

In the spring arctic foxes give birth to babies called whelps or pups. The caring parents work together to raise them. While the female remains in the den nursing the litter, her mate hunts.

After the young are weaned and no longer need their mother's milk, the female helps her mate hunt. To feed a litter of ten whelps, the parents must kill about thirty lemmings a day. By the time a litter of this size is almost ready to leave the den, adult foxes must feed them over one hundred lemmings a day!

The coats of arctic foxes become reddish brown in summer, as shown above.

A hungry arctic fox has found a muskox carcass on which to munch.

Finding food

Arctic foxes that live near the coast eat the carcasses of seals killed by polar bears. Occasionally foxes kill newborn seal pups themselves. Lemmings are the main food source of inland arctic foxes. They may bear over a dozen babies when there is a large lemming population. When there are few lemmings, foxes only give birth to a few whelps. Having a large litter during times of little food would mean certain starvation for a fox family.

Eating what is available

Animals that live in the Arctic cannot depend on a constant supply of food, and sometimes the foods that they prefer are not available. Despite these problems, many animals are able to live in the far north because they are opportunistic feeders. Opportunistic feeders are not picky eaters. They eat many different kinds of food as the opportunity arises. If the hunting is good, an arctic fox eats lemmings but, if there are no lemmings, this opportunistic feeder will not hesitate to eat the remains of a muskox.

The arctic wolf

For thousands of years people have feared and hated the wolf. They believed that wolves threatened people's lives and those of their livestock. Only recently have scientists proven that the wolf is a misunderstood animal.

Wolves are actually very social and affectionate creatures. They nuzzle, play together, and sometimes pounce on pack members to scare them for fun. They hunt mostly in wilderness areas and prefer to avoid people. A wolf will not attack a human being unless it is sick with rabies, starving, or forced to defend itself. Being a predator of animals is the wolf's natural role in the food chain.

Intelligent hunters

Arctic wolves eat a variety of small rodents such as lemmings, rabbits, and ground squirrels. They also hunt together in packs, stalking and killing caribou or muskoxen. Wolves usually attack the old, young, or sick animals in a herd because these are the slower and weaker targets. This helps keep the herds healthy, and it ensures that these animals will not live to mate or spread their diseases.

Wolves are not particularly fast hunters, but they are efficient. They are intelligent and cooperate with one another during hunting expeditions. Sometimes wolves take turns chasing an animal until their prey is too tired to run anymore. On other occasions they might force their prey into places from which there is no escape.

Family ties

Wolf families live together and remain very close. Most wolf packs are made up of a male, a female, their pups, and other related adults. Each pack lives and hunts within its own area or territory. The members of a wolf pack mark their territory by urinating frequently on its boundaries. If other wolves enter, a fight sometimes results.

Tending the young

In the spring the female wolf prepares a den in which she gives birth to an average litter of six pups. During the warm arctic summer the pups play while their parents leave to hunt with the other members of the wolf pack. Some of the wolves stay behind to look after the pups. After killing their prey, the parent wolves eat more than they need. They return to their pups and regurgitate the fresh meat that is still undigested in their stomachs. The pups eat these ready-made meals until they are old enough to kill their own prey.

The husky

One of the best-known arctic animals is the husky. Not only is the husky a faithful friend, but also a valuable working dog. It can pull a sledge faster and farther than any other dog and is well furred to withstand the bitter cold. A team of huskies often costs as much as a new snowmobile but, once bought, it is very economical. While on the trapline, dogs eat meat scraps or fish but, if necessary, they can go without food for several days.

Part arctic wolf, the husky is a strong, intelligent animal that can find its way home through winter darkness and blizzard conditions. In a desperate situation, when sledge riders are lost or stranded, they must sometimes kill one of their dogs to avoid starvation. They only do this when their own lives are at stake, however. No one likes the idea of killing a loyal worker!

a husky

Lucky hopes that one day this little puppy will be the lead dog of his dog team!

53

The wolverine

The wolverine has been called a glutton, a trouble-maker, and a ferocious predator. Some people even believe that it is the animal behind the abominable snowman legends. A cloud of mystery surrounds the wolverine because this animal likes to be alone and is rarely seen by people. Recent studies have shown that the wolverine does not gorge itself on food and is not any more ferocious than an angry red squirrel.

Mating season is the only time of year that wolverines get together. Once mating has occurred, couples go their separate ways. Several months later mother wolverines make dens in rocky caves or beneath the roots of fallen trees. In March or April they have from two to five cubs. Wolverines do not breed until they are four years old. Most other arctic animals mate and have young long before this because they mature more rapidly than wolverines. Maturing late may account for the low wolverine population.

An omnivore's diet

The wolverine is the largest member of the weasel family and, like other weasels, it is an omnivore that feeds on a variety of animal and plant foods. In summer it eats blueberries, ground squirrels, and birds' eggs. In winter it hunts small animals but spends most of its time as a scavenger, feeding on the carcasses of caribou, seals, and even whales.

Bounding along

The wolverine is known for its big feet and loping gait. As it runs, its four furry feet hit the ground all at once. These furry feet tend to slow the animal down in the summer, but they are a great advantage in the winter. When the wolverine chases a caribou, moose, or other large animal in the deep snow, it can move quickly, whereas the prey exhausts itself. Thanks to its snowshoe feet, the wolverine is able to bound along on top of the snow and kill stranded animals.

The ermine

The ermine is another member of the weasel family. In the summer its long, lean body is covered in a coat of short dark brown fur. In the winter its coat turns to a snowy white color except for the black tip on its tail. In the past ermine furs and tails decorated the robes of royalty. Today ermines are still bred so that their pelts can be used to make coats. Ermine farmers of the Siberian Arctic make a good living raising these animals for their pelts.

Ermines make their homes in underground holes that have been dug out by other burrowing animals. Mother ermines make a cozy nursery lined with the fur from other animals. Their young grow quickly and are able to have families of their own in less than a year!

Night hunters

The ermine is an efficient hunter that preys on other small animals and birds. Its excellent sense of smell allows it to expertly sniff out its prey during the dark arctic nights. When killing its prey, the ermine pounces on it and bites it at the back of the neck. It then wraps its snakelike body around the victim to ensure that it cannot escape.

A fragile world

The arctic ecosystem is different from the ecosystems of more southerly regions. There are fewer species of animals because only a few species are able to withstand long periods of freezing cold and total darkness. Battling severe winter blizzards and changes in the environment is not the only challenge facing these animals, however. They must now also cope with pollution. Winds carry polluted air north from southern mines and factories. Harmful substances such as metal dust work their way into the food chain. Animals browsing for food on the ground or drinking surface water take in these pollutants and pass them on to the creatures that eat them.

The severe cold does not allow bacteria to break down litter that is thrown onto the tundra. Garbage that would decay in several months in more southern areas could take many years to decay in the Arctic.

Any big or sudden changes to the few species that exist in the Arctic can cause whole populations to decline or die off. The whole world must care about the Arctic because, once it is spoiled, this natural area and its wildlife will be gone forever. The Arctic belongs to you, too. Learn more about it and make others understand the importance of preserving one of our last wilderness areas and its animals!

Glossary

baleen - Part of the feeding system of toothless whales. Triangular-shaped plates that hang from the whales' jaws that collect marine creatures as the whales take in water.

camouflage - A way of disguising with colors or patterns that makes objects blend in with their surroundings.

carnivore - A creature that eats meat.

crustacean - One of a large number of creatures with a hard outer shell that lives in water.

dorsal fin - The fin on or near the back of a whale or fish.

ecosystem - The interacting community of plants and animals and the surroundings in which they live.

endangered - Close to becoming extinct.

Inuit - Native peoples who live in the Canadian Arctic and Greenland. Also a general name used for the native peoples who used to be called Eskimos.

krill - Small marine crustaceans.

lichen - A non-flowering plant that grows close to the ground and is found in northern regions.

migration - The act of moving from one area to another during certain seasons or following the availability of food.

molting - The act of shedding hair, feathers, skin, or a shell in preparation for new growth.

parasite - A plant or animal that lives in or on another creature and relies on it completely as a food source.

phytoplankton - Simple marine plants.

plankton - Water plants and animals that float or drift, rather than swim in the water.

pod - A group of whales that live or travel together.

predator - An animal that eats other animals.

prey - An animal that is hunted and eaten by another animal.

sedge - A grasslike plant with blades that are solid rather than hollow.

tundra - A treeless, flat region.

wean - To teach a baby mammal to eat foods other than its mother's milk.

zooplankton - Tiny marine animals.

Index

Acknowledgments

Front cover photo: Animals Animals/Breck P. Kent
Back cover and title page photos: Jerome Knap, William Belsey
Photo Credits: Janet Foster/Masterfile, pages 4, 14, 18, 21; Health and Welfare, pages 6, 7 (top), 53 (top); Anonymous/Masterfile, pages 7 (bottom), 8, 23, 42; Wayne Lynch/Masterfile, page 9; Animals Animals/J. Cooke, page 10 (bottom); William Belsey, pages 11, 33; John Fowler/Valan Photos, page 13; George Calef/Masterfile, pages 20, 32; SSC-Photocentre-ASC/Photo by: Jean-Louis Frund, pages 24 (top), 48; Jerome Knap, pages 24 (center), 50; Barrett and MacKay/Masterfile, page 24 (bottom); Bob Wood, pages 25 (top), 29; G. Meszaros/Masterfile, page 25 (center); Roy Morsch/Masterfile, page 25 (bottom); Barry Griffiths, pages 26, 27 (bottom), 37, 38-39, 40 (top), 49 (bottom); L. L. Rue III/Masterfile, page 27 (top); Animals Animals/Alan G. Nelson, page 28; Ken Faris, pages 30, 44, 53 (bottom); SSC-Photocentre-ASC/Photo by: Pat Morrow, page 31; Finland Tourist Board, page 40 (bottom); D. Paterson/Health and Welfare, page 43; B. and C. Calhoun/Masterfile, page 45; SSC-Photocentre-ASC/Photo by: George Hunter, page 46; Krasenann/Valan Photos, page 47; SSC-Photocentre-ASC/Photo by: J. D. Taylor, page 49 (bottom); Freeman Patterson/Masterfile, page 51; Bill Mason, page 52; Esther Schmidt/Valan Photos, page 54; Wayne Lankinen/Valan Photos, page 55; Ted Grant/Masterfile, page 56.
Illustrations: Glen Loates, page 10 (top); Elaine Macpherson, pages 16, 27, 41; Halina Below-Spada, page 34-35; Susan Laurie-Bourque, pages 36, 37.